ABOUT THE AUTHOR

Cynthia Holt Cummings, a resident of West Bloomfield, Michigan, was born in West Boylston, Massachusetts. Upon graduation from Massachusetts General Hospital School for Nurses, she joined the hospital's 6th General Hospital reserve unit as a second lieutenant in the Army Nurse Corps. Shortly after World War II began, the hospital unit departed for active duty, spending thirty-three months in North Africa and Italy.

She later married Richard Howe Cummings. Their son Roger Holt Cummings, named after her youngest brother, an Air Force gunner killed during the war, is married to Buff with two children... David and Julie.

With warm friendly thoughts.
Fondly,
Cynthia Holt Cummings

CHRISTMAS LOVE

Poetry by

Cynthia Holt Cummings

Illustrations by

Danna Clark

ABOUT THE ARTIST

Danna Mertz Clark was born and raised in Adams County, Colorado. Her early interest in art was greatly supported by her parents, and further developed with a fondly remembered high school teacher.

She makes her home and studio on a horse farm in Oxford, Michigan, with her husband Don and four year old son, Sean. Weekends are shared with step children, Cassidy and Erin.

Cynthia and Danna dedicate this book to the children.... David, Julie, Cassidy, Erin and Sean.

Copyright 1984, Holt Peterson Press
Printed in the United States
First printing 1984

Holt Peterson Press
P.O. Box 3354
Farmington Hills, MI 48018

Other books by Holt Peterson Press:

Christmas Ribbons

first printing 1979
second printing 1980
third printing 1981
fourth printing 1982
fifth printing 1983

Christmas Memories

first printing 1982

CHRISTMAS LOVE

Love for Little Children

It's our love for little children
That keeps Christmas all year long.
As we listen to their laughter,
We can make a Christmas song.
As we take their hands and lead them,
All the days throughout the year,
We can show them that we love them,
And keep their love quite near.

Take a moment to remember,
Thoughts of love in this December.

Favorite Treasure

In the chest
Were all her treasures
Summer days had been such fun.
Tiny stones and soft bird feathers
She had saved them one by one.
Now at Christmastime once more,
She opened up the chest
And gave her favorite treasure
To the one she loved the best.

The trumpet sounds to praise God's name,
And the echo is heard in a candle's flame.

With your arms around the children
Tell the story once again
of the Savior, of his coming,
Bringing peace good will to men.

When Christmas Comes Each Year

It's the joy of children
The warmth of love
The many blessings
Beneath the star above
The many friends we know
The neighbors living near
That makes our lives so special
When Christmas comes each year.

The joy of living,
Is found in giving.

Toy soldier, take care of the children tonight,
Keep the star of peace glowing so bright.

Many Things

I love Christmas for many things
Trees, candles, angel wings.
Stars in the heavens,
Snow covered hills,
Little toy trains,
Dolls in their frills.

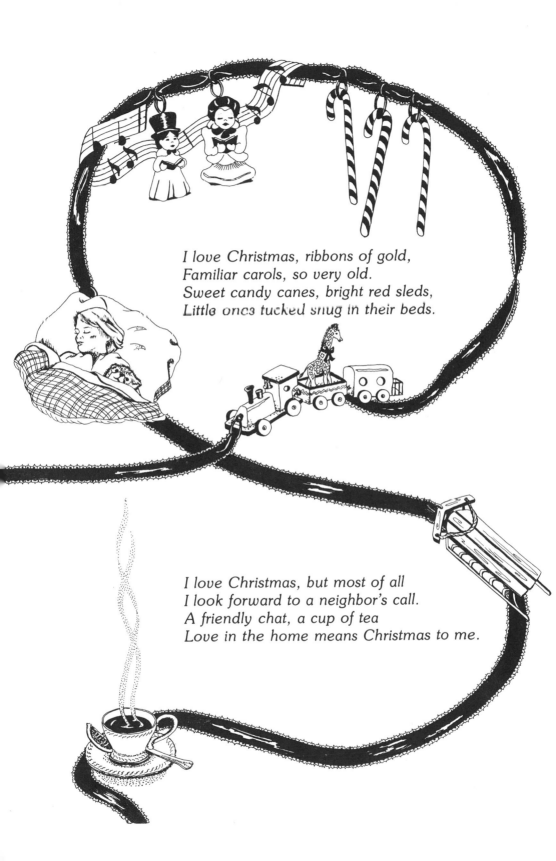

I love Christmas, ribbons of gold,
Familiar carols, so very old.
Sweet candy canes, bright red sleds,
Little ones tucked snug in their beds.

I love Christmas, but most of all
I look forward to a neighbor's call.
A friendly chat, a cup of tea
Love in the home means Christmas to me.

What Is It?

Is it the sparkle on the tree,
The green wreath on the door,
The present tied with ribbon red,
Or is it something more?
The cheery greeting when we meet
A friend along our way,
The crunch of snow beneath our feet,
The children in their play?
We ask ourselves,
What is it?
But in the end we know
It's our love for one another
That makes Christmas spirit glow.

Unaware

We sat around the table,
Love was always there.
We didn't even notice,
The gray streaks in her hair.
Her busy hands were making,
Sweet cakes for oven baking,
And on her face were wrinkles,
But we were unaware.
For sunshine filled the laughing room,
We didn't even know,
That love and sunshine disappear
When mothers have to go.

What Will I Give Her?

What will I give her for Christmas…
Long stem roses of brightest red
Or maybe a silver chain instead?
A white fur muff to warm her hands
Or books with stories of far off lands?
A music box that's filled with song
To show my love the whole day long?
What will I give her for Christmas…
I ask it over and over again
When I know that the answer
Is always the same,
I'll give her my heart to mend.

So simple this year, the gift that I give,
Joy in your heart for each day that you live.

Faith, Joy and Love

If love is in the stocking,
And joy is on the tree,
If faith is in the glowing star,
Then friendship is the key
To blessings in the coming year,
With faith and joy and love quite near.

Gather love on Christmas Day
And let your heart give it away.

When hearts hold love to give away,
Joy fills each home on Christmas Day.

Greetings

In the hearts of little children,
Love is always waiting there
For someone with understanding,
Just to let them know you care.
Once again we send our greetings
To all both near and far,
Gathering love for all the children
Beneath the glowing star.

Christmas Lullaby

Cozy and warm from the winter snow,
She remembers the star with its Christmas glow.
She thinks of the days and years ahead,
As she tucks the children into bed.

I'll give them love and teach them to pray,
I'll show them how to give smiles away.
I'll help them build castles in the sand,
And teach them to give a helping hand.
I'll let them know what it is to share,
So someone will know that they really care.
I'll help them grow in the kindly way,
And give them some happiness every day.

This is the lullaby she sings tonight,
With the star high overhead.
This is her Christmas lullaby,
As she tucks the children into bed.

I Tie My Love With Ribbons

In the glow of Christmas candles
And the stars that shine above,
I bring you season's greetings
With my ribboned gift of love.
In the joyous sound of voices
Singing carols in the snow,
I take your hand and tell you
Of my love that seems to grow.
With Christmas years behind us
And Christmas years ahead,
I tie my love with ribbons
In the shade of Christmas red.

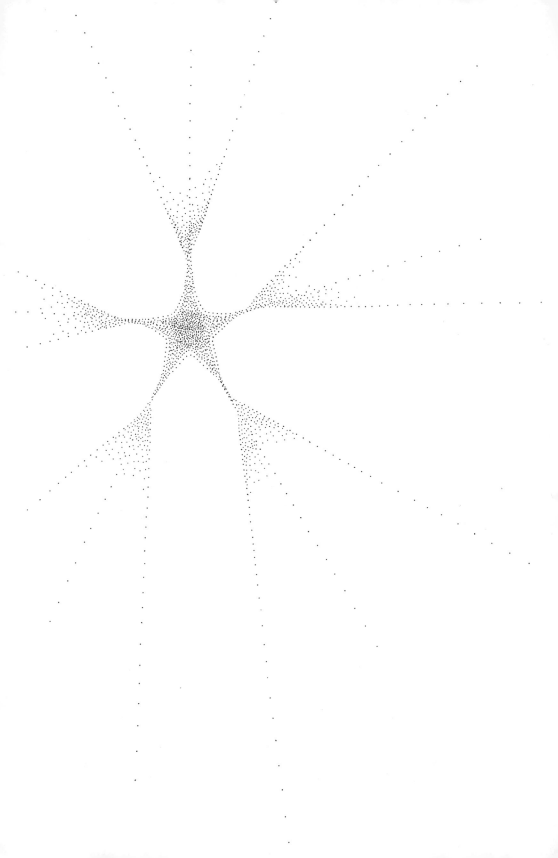

Peace be in the hearts of men,
Spreading Christmas love again.

Chiming

I hear them ringing in the hills
And in the valley too.
Church bells chiming carols
Oh so old, but oh so new.
Telling of the Holy Birthday
Of a child born long ago.
Church bells chiming, chiming, chiming,
All across the winter snow.

Christmas is wrapping each gift with care,
Bowing your head and saying a prayer.

How Much I Love You

I've done many things for Christmas;
I've tied each present with bow,
But there's one other thing
I wanted to tell you,
How much I love you,
But I think you know.

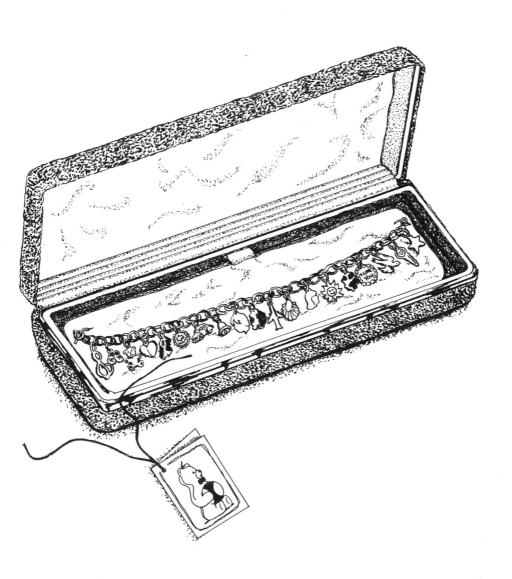

Christmas Gift

A chain of love I'll give to you
With trinkets old and trinkets new.
Some are silver - some are gold
But tucked there in between,
Are bits of tin and shiny brass
And pieces made of crystal glass.
For life holds joys and sorrows too
As years go quickly by;
Each helps to make love stronger
Reasons never tell us why.
Joy and sorrow are all a part
To make love stronger in our heart.
A chain of love I'll give to you
With trinkets old and trinkets new.

Jack Frost

By the light of a star he paints at night
In winter cold when the earth is white.
Delicate lace on the window pane
While Christmas is filling the world again.
Icicle brushes in his sack
A snowflake coat upon his back
A ribboned scarf of winter wind
This is the way I picture him.
Delicate lace, painted with care,
Jack Frost leaves his gift
For all to share.

Christmas Carol

I can hear you scampering little mouse
High in the attic of this old house.
What are you looking for?
Is it still there?
The tiny toy soldier,
The old rocking chair,
Is it the tinsel to trim the tree?
Or cards from old friends
In a trunk with a key?
The train is still packed,
The drum doesn't beat,
And I know little mouse
There is nothing to eat.
The attic door opened,
With the chime of a bell;
Santa had come
With your secret to tell.
As he opened his pack,
The little bell chime
Told me again,
It was Christmastime.

So when it is Christmas,
I listen once more
For your scampering feet
On the old attic floor.
And soon I can hear,
I know it so well,
Your own Christmas carol,
The chime of a bell.

Christmas Is

Christmas is a present
Tied with red bow
A bright glowing star
A field white with snow.
A tree that is green,
Trimmed with tinsel and gold,
Christmas is love,
For a stocking to hold.

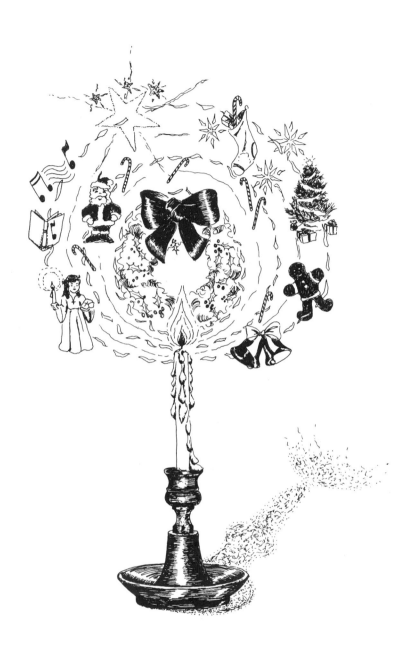

Christmas memories fill the night,
Woven into candlelight.

Prayer

Between two hands
A prayer is said
Before we tuck her into bed.
Lord help us share
Our love each day
With those we meet along our way.

Christmas Cloud

Christmas Cloud, a jollyman
High up in the sky,
All summer long looked for shade
As other clouds passed by.
He must keep cool to make the snow
When winter rolled around,
So he rested in the shade
When'ere it could be found.
When autumn leaves began to fall
This was his busiest time of all.

One night he felt the cold, cold wind
It blew and blew and blew.
All the little children
Felt the cold wind too.
Skates and skis would soon come out
From closets down below;
Shovels would be dancing
Up and down the walks in snow.

As neighbors shared their greetings
In Merry Christmas talk,
Christmas Cloud was busy
Letting snowflakes drop.
A beautiful sight to see
This winter world of snow;
On every graceful green fir tree
Christmas lights began to glow.

Christmas Cloud heard voices
All across the town:
Merry, Merry Christmas
Greeted snowflakes falling down.
Along with Christmas greetings
He heard them once again
Wishing friend and neighbor
Peace on earth-good will to men.

Bless the children in their beds,
And leave your love beside their sleds.